DISCLAIMER:

This book is intended to empower mommas to enjoy themselves throughout the trials and tribulations of motherhood. We are not advocating intoxicated child-rearing.

Please drink responsibly.

A.K.A. Karen, calm down.

VMH Publishing
Atlanta, GA | New York, NY
vmhpublishing.net

Manufactured in the United States of America

Hardback ISBN: 979-8-9865891-9-0
Paperback ISBN: 979-8-9865891-8-3

10 9 8 7 6 5 4 3 2 1

Publisher's Note:
The publisher is not responsible for the content of this book nor websites, or social media pages (or their content) that are not owned by the publisher.

POUR PARENTING

A TRUE MOTHERS SURVIVAL GUIDE

Written by
Lindsay Davis
Amanda Cox
Katie Anastassakis

Illustrated by:
Marisa Randles

DEDICATION

This book is dedicated to the Moms out there with the weight of the world on their shoulders. No matter WHAT your path or current position looks like, know that wine will not get you to the finish line...

But it sure can help along the way!

INTRODUCTION

Motherhood is a complex blend of emotional fulfillment and mental anxiety. It's a blur of stress between snacks, meltdowns, homework, forcing dinner down their throats, and screaming, "FINE! I DON'T CARE! You can STAAAARVE!" Homework should be done by now but is put off until after dinner when everyone is reenergized.

I look around and see the laundry that needs to be folded, the lunches need to be packed (but let's be honest, that'll happen last minute or tomorrow morning. Every. Time.), dishes in the sink and work prep for the next day.

The ONLY thing that calms my mind during these moments, and maybe even makes it a bit more enjoyable, is a big ol' glass of wine. I didn't get to the farmers market to concoct my charcuterie board so this over-poured glass is going with the kid's half-eaten pizza crust.

This is my "me time."

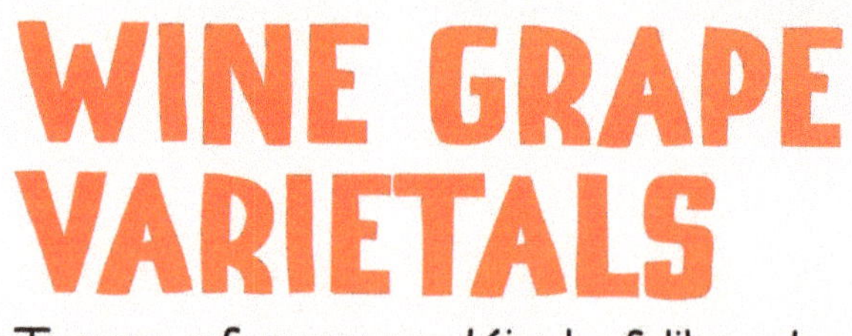

WINE GRAPE VARIETALS

Types of grapes. Kind of like cheese-you have cheddar, mozzarella, provolone, gouda... in the end it's all cheese. But they taste different! Some basic, some fancy and bougie.

To Moms,
they all taste delicious.

RICH WHITE

Chardonnay
Voignier
Roussane
Marsanne

SWEET WHITE

Moscato
Gewurztraminer
Malvasia
Resling

DRY WHITE

Sauvignon Blanc
Pinot Grigio/Gris
Albarino
Riesling
Malvasia

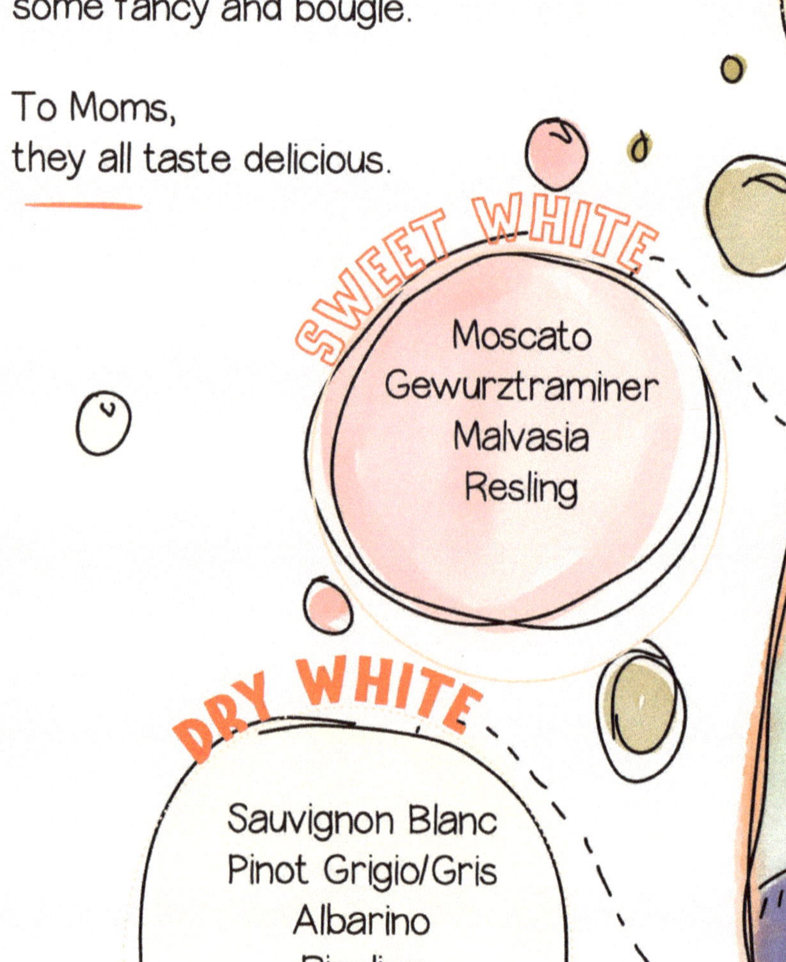

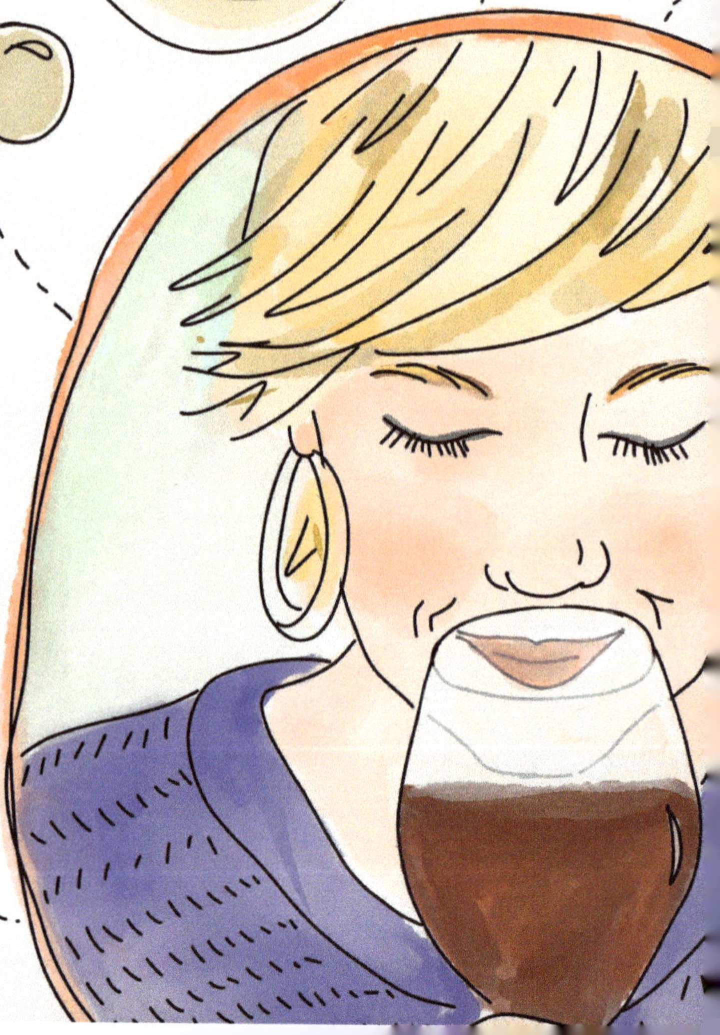

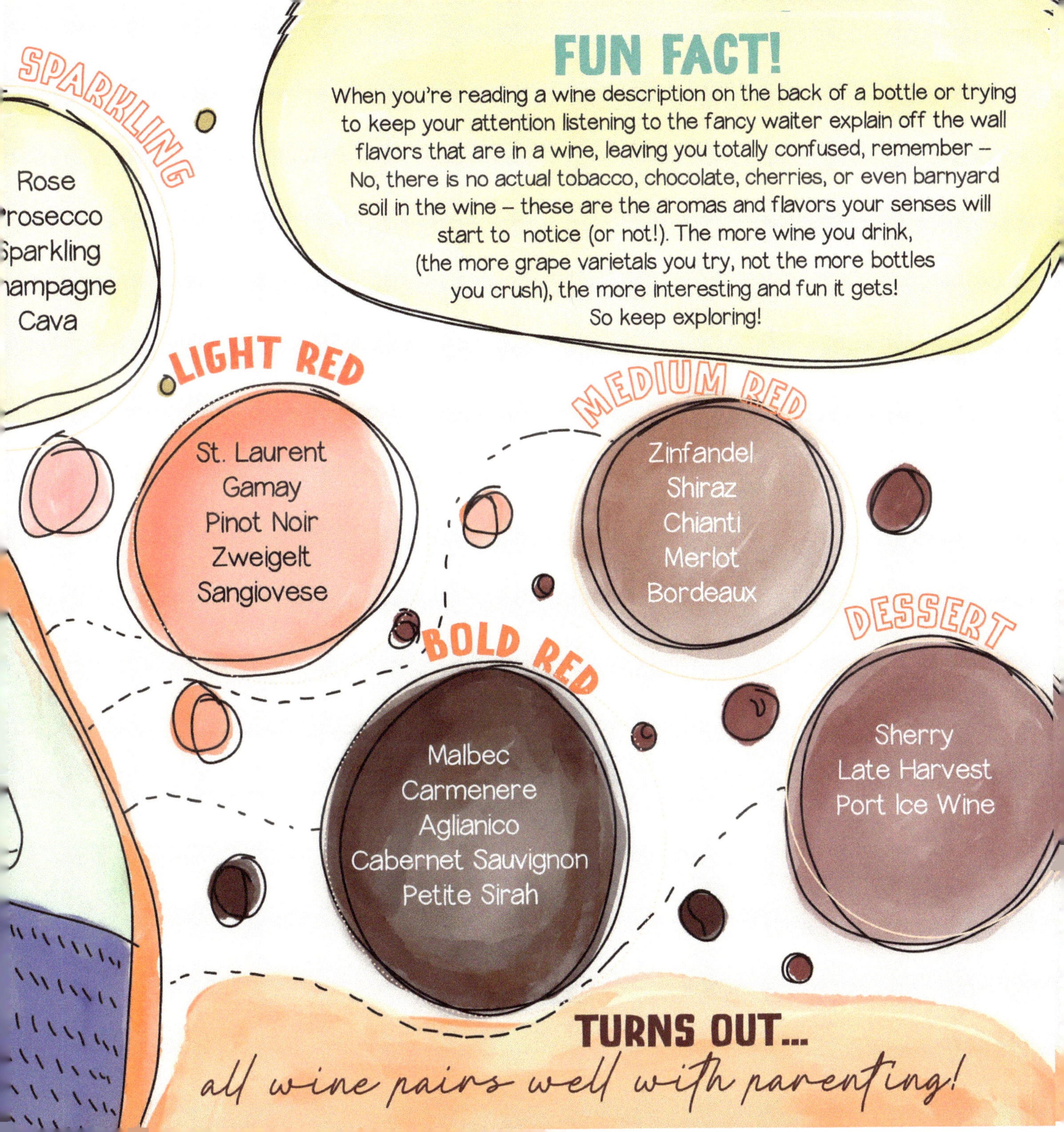
SPARKLING
Rose
rosecco
Sparkling
hampagne
Cava
FUN FACT!
When you're reading a wine description on the back of a bottle or trying to keep your attention listening to the fancy waiter explain off the wall flavors that are in a wine, leaving you totally confused, remember – No, there is no actual tobacco, chocolate, cherries, or even barnyard soil in the wine – these are the aromas and flavors your senses will start to notice (or not!). The more wine you drink, (the more grape varietals you try, not the more bottles you crush), the more interesting and fun it gets! So keep exploring!
LIGHT RED
St. Laurent
Gamay
Pinot Noir
Zweigelt
Sangiovese
MEDIUM RED
Zinfandel
Shiraz
Chianti
Merlot
Bordeaux
BOLD RED
Malbec
Carmenere
Aglianico
Cabernet Sauvignon
Petite Sirah
DESSERT
Sherry
Late Harvest
Port Ice Wine
TURNS OUT...
all wine pairs well with parenting!

You finally muster up the courage to clean out your car. Everything is going smoothly until you unearth the major contributor to your vehicle's smell.

A three-week-old sippy cup full of now partially congealed milk discovered in the back of the minivan is best with a full-bodied California Chardonnay with creamy buttery notes to offset the rancid dairy smell you just gagged off. Don't bother trying to save the sippy cup because nothing short of cleansing it with fire will ever make it clean again.

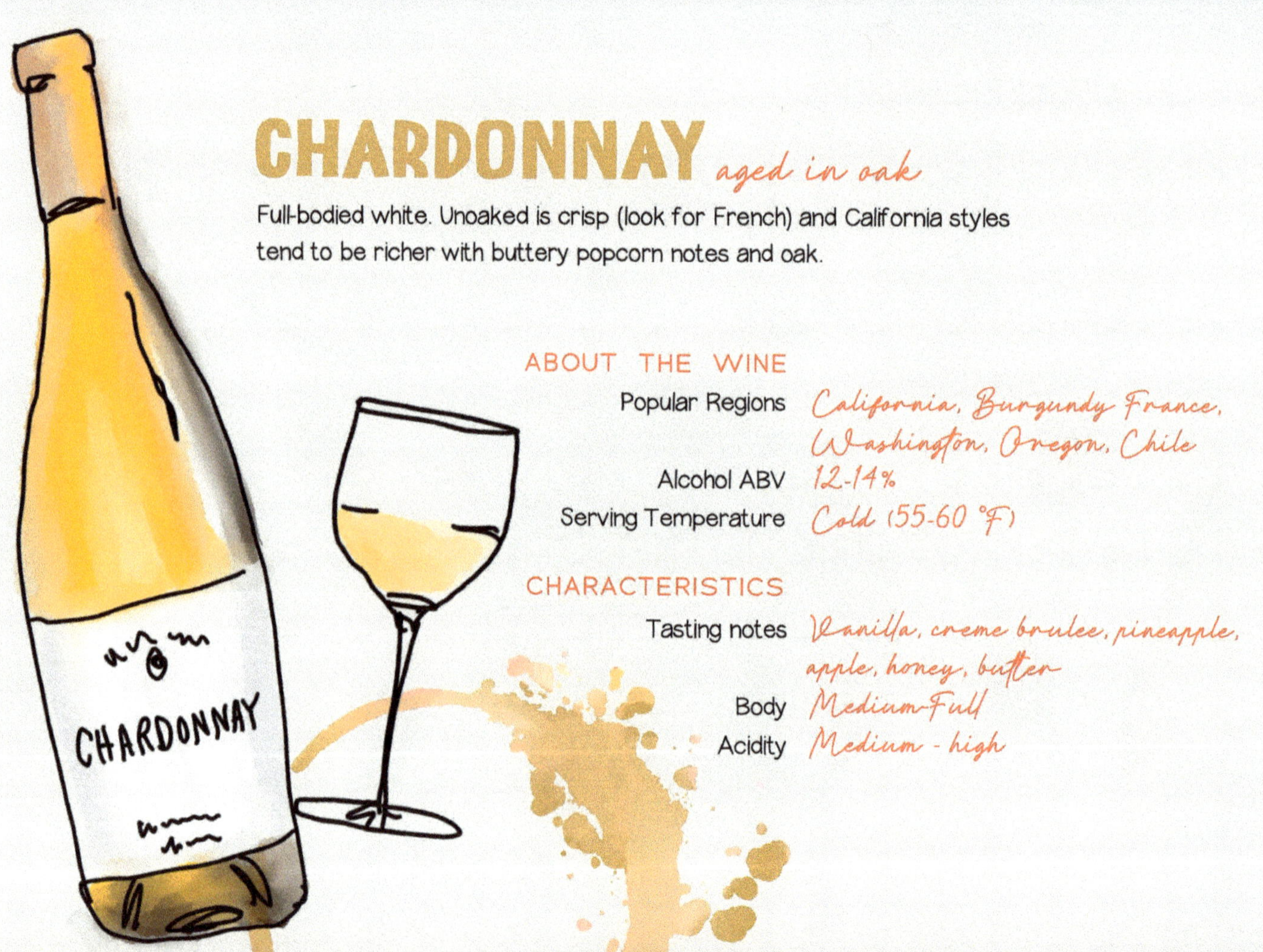

CHARDONNAY *aged in oak*

Full-bodied white. Unoaked is crisp (look for French) and California styles tend to be richer with buttery popcorn notes and oak.

ABOUT THE WINE

Popular Regions	*California, Burgundy France, Washington, Oregon, Chile*
Alcohol ABV	*12-14%*
Serving Temperature	*Cold (55-60 °F)*

CHARACTERISTICS

Tasting notes	*Vanilla, creme brulee, pineapple, apple, honey, butter*
Body	*Medium-Full*
Acidity	*Medium - high*

Realizing you have not stopped all day to eat a meal, you find a stale cheese ball wedged in the couch and you figure, "why not?"

Your regrettable dining decision goes perfectly with an undervalued $9 Chilean Cabernet which will pair perfectly with the overly chewy cheddar... just make sure to pick off the dog hair stuck to anything else you find on your hunt for subpar snacks.

CABERNET SAUVIGNON

Full-bodied, tannins (mouth drying), dark fruit, and tobacco.
Perfect with a fatty steak.

ABOUT THE WINE

Popular Regions	California, Bordeaux France, Washington, Chile, Spain
Alcohol ABV	13-15%
Serving Temperature	Cold (55-60 °F)

CHARACTERISTICS

Tasting notes	Dark berry fruit, Vanilla, bell pepper, tobacco, plum
Body	Full
Acidity	Medium

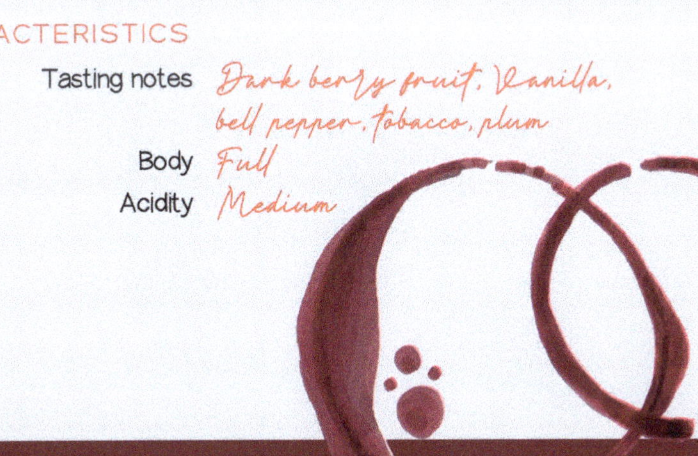

Bathing your kid, you turn to get a towel and you hear it: grunting. You turn back around in terror to find your darling baby angel attempting to play in their own self-made poop soup. Your child is going to require a thorough kitchen sink hose-down, and your tub a lot of bleach.

Keeping your nose in a glass of California Zinfandel that has strong fruit and tobacco notes will help keep your stomach from turning at your child's latest culinary fiasco. Also, it's about 15% alcohol, so you can dull the memory until you are ready to laugh at it one day.

ZINFANDEL

Zinfandel is red. Not to be confused with the pink colored "White Zinfandel" which is very sweet.Red Zinfandel is typically high in alcohol and can be a little sweet, with smokey notes.

ABOUT THE WINE

Popular Regions: California

Alcohol ABV: 13-16%

Serving Temperature: Room Temperature (65 °F)

CHARACTERISTICS

Tasting notes: Dark fruit, smoke, raisin

Body: Full

Acidity: Low

BleacH

1
2

In a moment of weakness, you give your child slime just one more time, only to be met 5 minutes later with a fat glob of it in their hair. After "yeeting" that clump of slime hair into the trash and beginning the arduous of cleaning up, be sure to pair your questionable decision-making skills with a crisp glass of New Zealand Sauvignon Blanc.

The grassy notes and hint of green color in your glass seem fitting with the neon green slime that will be forever stuck in your carpet.

SAUVIGNON BLANC

Crisp and acidic. Great with food like salads and fish. New Zealand tends to be more grapefruit flavors while others show notes of tropical fruit.

ABOUT THE WINE

Popular Regions	France, California, New Zealand, Chile
Alcohol ABV	11.5-14%
Serving Temperature	Cold (45-50 °F)

CHARACTERISTICS

Tasting notes	Pear, grapefruit, green herbs, peach
Body	Light
Acidity	High

You begrudgingly drag your hind end out of the house to go grocery shopping and cave on getting the big obnoxious buggy that looks like a car, knowing dang well that your kid won't stay in it for long.

Two minutes later, your "little helper" is running up and down the aisles as if they have never been in a store before. Be sure to swing by the wine section and pick up a nice box of red blend that doesn't even tell you what grapes might be in it. Just stick a straw in it like a juice box because you're done, babe. Accept it.

RED BLEND

Could be a blend of many or few varietals. Typically fruit-forward and easy drinking. Should pair perfectly with pizza night and BBQ. And since no air gets in, it'll last for months once opened! FYI - that opened bottle of cabernet on the top of your fridge that you opened two months ago needs to be dumped down the sink already!

ABOUT THE WINE

Popular Regions	*California*
Alcohol ABV	*13-15%*
Serving Temperature	*Room Temperature (65 °F)*

CHARACTERISTICS

Tasting notes	*Depending on grape varietals, typically fruit forward, dark berries, smoke*
Body	*Medium-Full*
Acidity	*Medium*

SAUCE
RICE CAKES
SNACKS
CHIPS
DESSERTS
DRINKS
CEREAL
BAKED GOODS
BAKING
FLOUR
SAVE $2.00
Detox Juices
NOW AVAILABLE!
Sale 30% off
SALE

When you step out of the shower - only to be met by your very curious kindergartener who then proceeds to hammer you with a million questions like the press after winning a football game. All inquiries involve body parts you're DEFINITELY not ready to discuss. As you hastily try to grab clothes and get dressed in the closet, make a mental note to pop open that bottle of Moscato.

Since it's most likely morning time, let's keep it classy and be responsible with a wine that has only 5% alcohol. Choose one with extra sweet notes of peaches and count it as a fruit for breakfast.

MOSCATO

A very sweet Italian white wine. The alcohol levels are much lower (about 5%) because the process of fermenting the natural sugar in the grape into alcohol is halted halfway through. Pairs great with dessert, or on its own if you like to sip on something sweet.

ABOUT THE WINE

Popular Regions *Italy, California*

Alcohol ABV *5-8%*

Serving Temperature *Cold (50 °F)*

CHARACTERISTICS

Tasting notes *honeysuckle, orange, peach*

Body *light*

Acidity *medium-high*

Daylight savings time's new bedtime schedule is wreaking havoc on your world. After your insomniac child finally passes out, just grab a bottle of bubbles. We suggest Prosecco if you don't want to use up this week's grocery budget. But, if you want to drink like the Queen you are, pop that bottle of French Champagne.

You deserve it, sis.

PROSECCO

A wine region in Veneto, Italy is famous for producing a light, refreshing, and affordable sparkling wine. Prosecco is made from the Glera grape. It is typically more of a value because of the lower costs involved to produce it. It is not aged in oak. Prosecco is fermented to sparkling in a tank, whereas Champagne or the "Traditional Method" is fermented in the bottle. Prosecco is the perfect choice for Mimosas!

ABOUT THE WINE

Popular Regions — *Italy*

Alcohol ABV — *11-13%*

Serving Temperature — *Very Cold (40-45 °F)*

CHARACTERISTICS

Tasting notes — *Lemon, apple, peach*

Body — *Light*

Acidity — *High*

i love
you
10:50

peas
CORN

When your body is a living, breathing jungle gym and your knees and back can't take much more amateur gymnastics, excuse yourself for a quick glass of Bordeaux. This will be a heavy glass of red that's a blend of cab and merlot. The cab eases the muscles and the merlot helps it all wash down and refreshes your spirit.

BORDEAUX

A wine region in the southwest of France. One of the most prestigious in the world. Bordeaux is typically made with the red varietals of Cabernet Sauvignon, Merlot, Cabernet Franc, and a few others. Commonly a blend. If you hear the term "Bordeaux style blend", you can usually bet it's a denser full-bodied red made with the makeup of Cabernet and Merlot.

ABOUT THE WINE

Popular Regions *Bordeaux France, California*

Alcohol ABV *13-15.5%*

Serving Temperature *Room Temperature (65 °F)*

CHARACTERISTICS

Tasting notes *Blackberry, Soil, Plum, Oak*

Body *Full*

Acidity *Medium*

Your Saturdays spent chauffeuring your children from one extracurricular activity to the next should always end with an extra cold glass of French Rose, particularly from the Provence region. This way, you can close your eyes on your front step and pretend you are in the South of France overlooking the Mediterranean and ignore the shrill screaming coming from inside.

That's not an "I'm bleeding" scream, they can work it out.

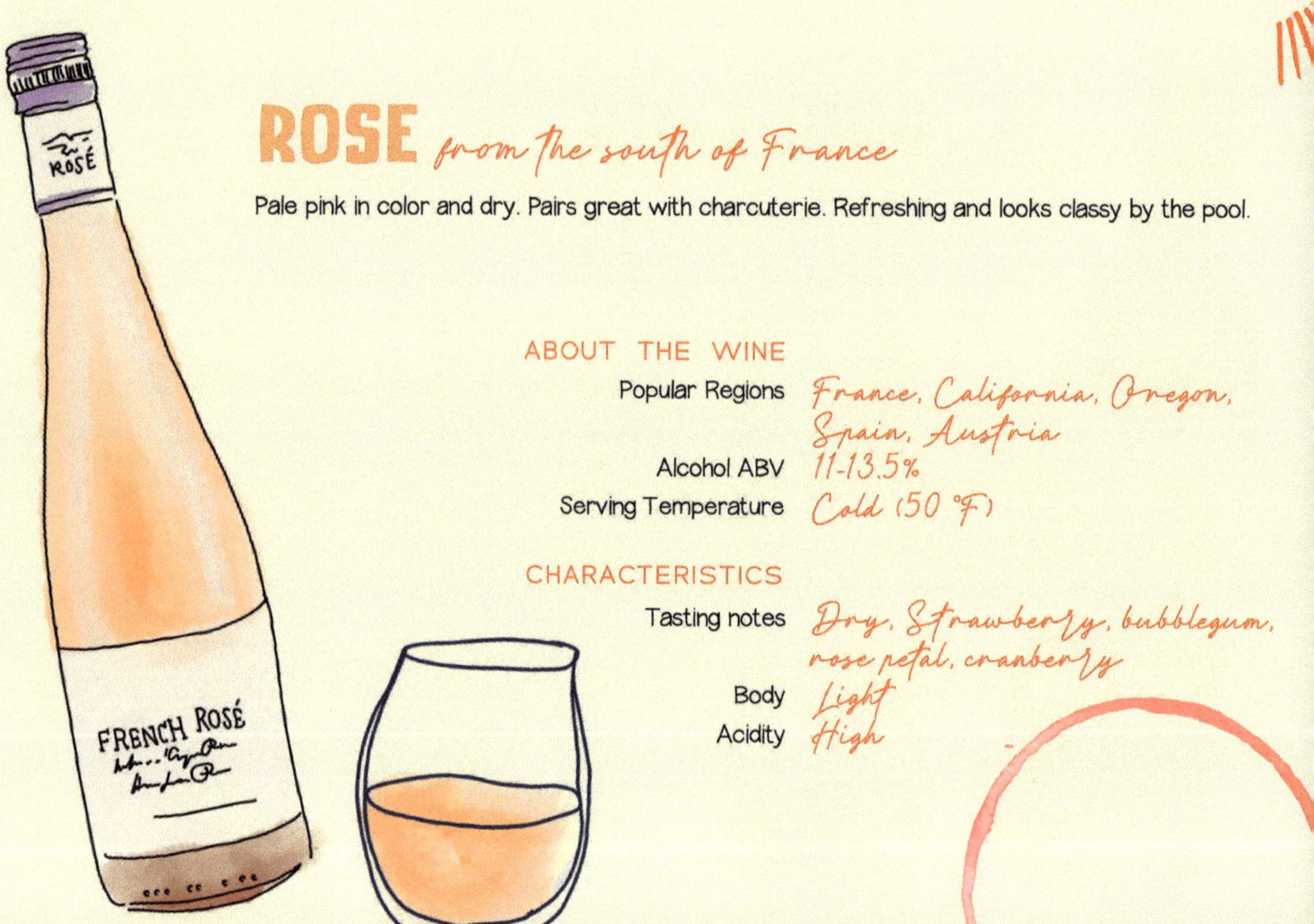

ROSE *from the south of France*

Pale pink in color and dry. Pairs great with charcuterie. Refreshing and looks classy by the pool.

ABOUT THE WINE

Popular Regions	France, California, Oregon, Spain, Austria
Alcohol ABV	11-13.5%
Serving Temperature	Cold (50 °F)

CHARACTERISTICS

Tasting notes	Dry, Strawberry, bubblegum, rose petal, cranberry
Body	Light
Acidity	High

WEEKLY MENU
MON- Meatloaf
Mashed Potatoes
G.BEANS CEREAL
TUES-TACOS
WEDS- Baked chicken
BROC, MAC'N CHEESE
THURS- Leftovers
FRI - PIZZA

All the menu planning in the world is wasted when you forget to take the meat out of the freezer for dinner, and all you're left with is nothing but cereal. Just know that your sugar-fused bowl of failure tastes a bit more like a win if you pour a glass of sweet German Riesling.

Rule of thumb: sweet always pairs well with sweet.

RIESLING

Typically on the sweet side from Germany. Dry from France. A little bit of both from the United States. Slightly sweet Reislings pair well with sushi and Asian dishes.

ABOUT THE WINE

Popular Regions	Germany, Washington, Australia
Alcohol ABV	7-10%
Serving Temperature	Cold (45-50 °F)

CHARACTERISTICS

Tasting notes	Honeysuckle, apple, vanilla, cantaloupe
Body	Light
Acidity	High

When you finally suck it up and attend to your mountain of laundry, prepare a nice, smooth glass of Oregon Pinot Noir. You may pay a few bucks more for Oregon, but the quality is worth the splurge. Take a sip and start binging your favorite show as you mindlessly fold until you can see your laundry chair again.

PINOT NOIR

One of the lightest red wines. Even better with a 10-minute chill in the fridge.

ABOUT THE WINE

Popular Regions	Burgundy & Loire FR, Chile, CA OR, Germany, New Zealand
Alcohol ABV	12-14%
Serving Temperature	Slightly chilled (55-60 °F)

CHARACTERISTICS

Tasting notes	Cherry, Raspberry, Mushroom, earth, violet, Vanilla
Body	Light-Medium
Acidity	High

Snack
tarts
Blueberry
120

When you break down and buy your kid's favorite snack in bulk just to be met with "Eww, I don't want that anymore!" less than a week into your purchase. Chase away the bitter feelings with a strong and extra fruity Petite Sirah which pairs well with your new army-sized snack fail.

PETITE SIRAH

Full-bodied, fruit-forward, and might leave you with purple lips. Pairs famously with ribs, but is also a good match for stinky cheese and wild game meats.

ABOUT THE WINE

Popular Regions	California
Alcohol ABV	13.5-14.5%
Serving Temperature	Room temperature (65 °F)

CHARACTERISTICS

Tasting notes	Jam, vanilla, blueberry, lavender
Body	Full
Acidity	Medium

Santa Clara Valley
AWARD WINNING
PETITE SIRAH SELECT
VINTAGE
2011

When your kids find the toy donation bags in the garage, take a big ol' swig of Albariño. It will be refreshing and crisp enough to throw back quickly as you wait the 5 minutes for them to be bored with them again. Next time, take them straight to the donation center instead of waiting for a better time, ya rookie!

ALBARIÑO *(or Alvariño)*

A refreshing and crisp Spanish white. In Portugal, "Alvariñho" is the common grape used in Vinho Verde wine. Vinho Verde typically has a slight spritz and is usually a little lower in alcohol with a hint of sweetness. The perfect mid-day sipper!

ABOUT THE WINE

Popular Regions	*Spain, Portugal (Alvariñho)*
Alcohol ABV	*11.5-12.5%*
Serving Temperature	*Cold (45-50 °F)*

CHARACTERISTICS

Tasting notes	*Nectarine, lemon, honeydew melon*
Body	*Light*
Acidity	*High*

AAAAHHHH!!!!!
NEW MERCH
SMASH THAT LIKE BUTTON!!
SUCH A NOOB!

Drown out the sounds of your kid's favorite YouTuber with an equally large glass of Tuscana Rosso. An affordable Italian Blend might lead to you talking with your hands and in a louder than normal voice - much like the videos your ears are assaulted by. Take nice big sips as you count down the minutes until the parental control time limit kicks in.

Seriously though, have they heard of an inside voice? It is LITERALLY at the lowest volume setting without being mute!

TUSCANA ROSSO

An affordable Italian blend typically made from the Sangiovese grape, as well as international varietals Cabernet Sauvignon and Merlot.

ABOUT THE WINE

Popular Regions	*Tuscany Italy*
Alcohol ABV	*12.5-14%*
Serving Temperature	*Slightly chilled (55-60 °F)*

CHARACTERISTICS

Tasting notes	*Cherry, plum, cedar*
Body	*Medium*
Acidity	*Medium to high*

ABOUT US

KATIE ANASTASSAKIS

author

FAVORITE WINE — OREGON PINOT NOIR

Katie Anastassakis (ana/sta/sakis) was born and raised in Ontario Canada, and moved to Birmingham, Alabama with her husband in 2010. She is a mother of 2: 10 year old daughter and an 8 year old son. Katie is a 9-5 wine sales rep and 24/7 mom. She's trying to figure out Southern-mom culture as she goes (bless her heart), while still staying true to her roots. She is a Certified Specialist in Wine, and loves to share her knowledge of vino with friends and family, while watching them discover new favorites.

AMANDA COX

author

FAVORITE WINE — PINOT NOIR OR WHITE ZINFANDEL

Amanda Cox is a sarcastic but loving wife and mother of two small girls aged 8 and 5. She is an avid lover of all things nerd and enjoys making people laugh at or with her. When she's not running around experiencing life with her loved ones, you can find her on the couch binge-watching her latest obsession with her unbreakable wine glass and the bag of chocolate she keeps hidden from the family.

LINDSAY DAVIS *author*

FAVORITE WINE A BOXED ROSE

Lindsay Davis is a mom of 3 kids, married for 10 years and CEO to one of the Inc 5000 Fastest Growing Companies in the country for 8 consecutive years. Her work schedule does not allot a ton of free time and any squeezed in is spent at some type of extra circulator activity with her children. Getting personal space and time : not a thing. So, she winds down with various wine favorites and obsessing over the latest Marvel cinematic adventure.

MARISA RANDLES *illustrator*

FAVORITE WINE CARMENERE OR MALBEC

Marisa Randles is a mother of 2 boys, ages 9 and 4. She is a global nomad, a plant based foodie, a coffee - wine - and nature lover, an activist, and an arts and music enthusiast. Her husband is a retired circus acrobat - they began raising their boys in Macau (China) and now, Mexico. She can be found adventuring with her kiddos, engaging in imaginary play, or watching her boys attempt various acrobatic stunts. Find her work at gypsy-jungle.com.

WE WANT THE QUIET

until we get it.

WE WANT LESS LAUNDRY

until it's gone.

WE WANT OUR BED BACK

until it's empty.

WE WANT OUR BODIES BACK

until we realize
their unimportance.

WE WANT TO SLEEP IN

until we can.

To this book's authors, being a mother is the most rewarding job and we wouldn't change a thing.

We want to encourage other mothers to introduce fun and humor into their caretaker role.

Our lives are non-stop chaos and this book has been our passion side project for years.

This project also took so long due to wine consumption during our writing sessions.

CABERNET SAUVIGNON
2019
PINOT NOIR
WINE OF CHILE
le BOXED WINE
CARDBORDEAUX
3 LITRES
MOSCATO
2021
RESERVE
RIESLING
ROSSO
PROSECCO
PINELLI
WINE O'CLOCK
WINE O'CLOCK
2014
Bordeaux

www.ingramcontent.com/pod-product-compliance
Ingram Content Group UK Ltd.
Pitfield, Milton Keynes, MK11 3LW, UK
UKHW061950290726
14090UKWH00021B/1165

9 798986 589183